John F. Kennedy

History Maker Bios

Jane Sutcliffe

BARNES & NOBLE

NEW YORK

Text © 2004 by Jane Sutcliffe
Illustrations © 2004 by Lerner Publications Company

This 2004 edition published by Barnes & Noble, Inc.,
by arrangement with Lerner Publications Company,
a division of Lerner Publishing Group, Minneapolis, MN.

Illustrations by Tim Parlin

Barnes & Noble, Inc.
122 Fifth Avenue
New York, NY 10011

ISBN-13: 978-0-7607-4034-7

Printed and bound in China

7   9   11   13   15   14   12   10   8

The quotes in this book have been drawn from many sources, and are assumed to
be accurate as quoted in their previously published forms. Although every effort has
been made to verify the quotes and sources, the publishers cannot guarantee their
perfect accuracy.

All websites and URLs in this book are current at the point of publication.
However, websites may be taken down and URLs may change after publication
without notice. The Publisher and the Author are not responsible for the content
contained in any specific website featured in this book, nor shall they be liable for
any loss or damage arising from the information contained in this book.

Table of Contents

INTRODUCTION

John F. Kennedy was the thirty-fifth president of the United States. Not everyone thought he would make a good president. Some people thought he was too young. Others said his religion was a problem.

President Kennedy worked hard to prove those people wrong. He led the United States during a dangerous time. He won the respect of the world. Then suddenly he was gone. His death shocked and saddened people everywhere.

This is his story.

1 A "MUCKER" GROWS UP

John F. Kennedy was not supposed to grow up to be president. His brother Joe was. At least that's what their father decided. And when Joseph Kennedy Sr. decided something, that was that.

John was born on May 29, 1917, in Brookline, Massachusetts. His father was a wealthy businessman. His mother was the daughter of the mayor of Boston.

John was named after his grandfather, John Fitzgerald. But everyone called him Jack. Jack was the second of nine Kennedy children. Joe was the first. All the Kennedy children liked sports and games. They raced sailboats and played rough games of touch football. They always played to win. "We don't want any losers around here," their father said. "In this family, we want winners."

The Kennedy family in 1932 (LEFT TO RIGHT): Bobby, Jack, Eunice, Jean, Mr. and Mrs. Kennedy, Patricia, Kathleen, Joe Jr., and Rosemary. Brother Teddy came along later.

Sometimes Jack couldn't play. He was sick much of the time. He had high fevers. His back hurt. His stomach bothered him.

Being sick so much made Jack skinny. Still, he was a handsome boy. He had blue eyes and thick sandy hair. When he laughed, his wide smile seemed to take up his whole face.

A TIE RACE

Jack and his brother Joe were always daring each other. Once they had a race around the block on their bikes. They set out in opposite directions. At the finish, they sped toward each other head-on. Neither would slow down or turn! The race ended in a bloody crash.

Jack needed twenty-eight stitches.

Jack (RIGHT) poses with a few of his fellow muckers.

When he was fourteen, Jack went away to high school. Joe was already there. The school had a lot of rules. Rules didn't bother Joe at all. He did well at school. But Jack was another story. He hated rules. He was always late to class. His room was a mess. And his grades were terrible.

The principal had a name for students like Jack. He called them "muckers." Jack didn't mind being called a mucker at all. In fact, he and his friends formed the Muckers Club. Soon there were over a dozen members.

Mostly, the boys just met in Jack's room and listened to music. But once a rumor went around the school. The Muckers were going to smuggle a pile of horse manure into a school dance. They were going to plop it right onto the dance floor!

The principal heard the rumor. That was the end of the Muckers Club. The principal called Jack's father to the school. Mr. Kennedy wasn't happy that his son was in trouble. But he was rather proud of Jack too. He saw that Jack had been a leader to the other boys.

Jack studied political science at Harvard. He also played football and competed on the swim team.

Jack (RIGHT) and Joe Jr. (LEFT) arrived in England with their father (CENTER) in the summer of 1938.

After he graduated from high school, Jack became a student at Harvard University. Then Jack's father got an important job in England. Jack took time off from Harvard to join his family there.

In 1939, Europe was headed for war. Jack traveled all over Europe. He wanted to see for himself what was going on. When he returned to Harvard, he wrote a long paper about what he had seen. Jack's professors liked his ideas. The paper helped Jack graduate from Harvard with honors.

Jack's father thought the paper would make a good book. He had friends who helped make it happen. In 1940, *Why England Slept* was published. Jack's book was a big hit.

By 1941, Jack was twenty-four. He was a Harvard graduate. He was a best-selling author and the son of a very wealthy man. Jack could have done just about anything. He decided to join the U.S. Navy. World War II was already being fought in Europe. Jack knew that soon the United States would have to join in too. He wanted to help his country when that happened.

2 PT-109

Bombs! Jack heard the word on the radio. Japanese planes had bombed the U.S. naval base at Pearl Harbor, Hawaii. The United States was at war.

Jack was sent to the Solomon Islands, in the Pacific Ocean. He took command of a small, flimsy wooden boat called a PT boat. The PT stood for "patrol torpedo." Jack's boat was *PT-109*.

When they got to the island, the men were exhausted. Jack was exhausted too. Even so, he swam back out to look for a rescue ship that night. He saw nothing.

For the next three days, Jack swam from island to island looking for help. At last, he met two natives. The natives agreed to carry a message for Jack. Of course, Jack didn't have any paper. So he used a knife to carve his message on a coconut.

Jack's unusual message worked. Six days after the crash, the crew was rescued. Jack was awarded the Navy and Marine Corps Medal for his bravery, but he hated being called a hero. He said, "The real heroes are not the men who return, but those who stay out there . . . two of my men included."

THE COCONUT IN THE WHITE HOUSE

Jack held on to his lucky coconut shell. When he became president, it sat on his desk in the White House.

Captain F. L. Conklin presents the Navy and Marine Corps Medal to Jack in 1944.

Jack's health had always been bad. After the shipwreck, it got worse. He was skinnier than ever. His back hurt so badly that he needed a cane to walk. The navy sent him home. In June 1944, Jack had surgery on his back. Then he went to his family's home to rest.

He was there when the Kennedys received terrible news. Jack's brother Joe had been killed in the war.

Everyone, especially Jack's father, had expected Joe to become a famous politician. Now Joe was gone. Mr. Kennedy began to focus on Jack instead. And Jack began to think about a life in politics.

THE CAMPAIGN TRAIL

In 1946, Massachusetts needed a new representative in the U.S. Congress. Jack's father wanted him to run for the office. Jack liked the idea too. There was only one problem. None of the voters knew who Jack was. So Jack's family went to work.

Jack's father used his money to buy advertising. Jack's mother and sisters held tea parties to introduce Jack to the voters.

Jack worked hardest of all. He went to factories, fire stations, and pool halls to meet voters. He gave speeches—hundreds of them. People liked his relaxed, easy way of speaking.

His father was surprised. He saw that Jack had a natural gift for politics.

When Jack first started running for office in 1946, he was a little shy. But he kept giving speeches. Soon it was clear that he had a passion for politics.

Jack won the election easily. The voters must have liked Representative Kennedy. They reelected him twice. In 1952, he ran for the U.S. Senate. When he won that election too, he became Senator Kennedy.

One night at a dinner party, Jack met Jacqueline Bouvier. "Jackie" was young, smart, and elegant. Jack had dated many pretty women. But he had never met anyone like Jackie. Jack and Jackie dated for almost one year. On September 12, 1953, they were married.

Jackie was beautiful and smart. She had gone to school in Paris and spoke four languages.

PROFILES IN COURAGE *quickly became a best-seller. Jack often signed copies of the book for his fans.*

The Kennedys had not been married long when Jack needed another operation on his back. This one went badly. Jack took months to recover. He used his time to write another book. The book told the stories of eight brave Americans, including John Quincy Adams and Sam Houston. Jack called it *Profiles in Courage.*

Jack and Jackie's first child, Caroline, was born in 1957. Caroline was a delight to her proud parents. They spent as much time with her as they could.

The book won an important award, the Pulitzer Prize. The book also earned Jack a lot of attention. In 1956, Jack was nearly picked as a candidate for vice president. He lost the vote. But he saw that with hard work, he could go even further. In January 1960, Jack announced that he would run for president of the United States.

Jack knew that he was not exactly a shoo-in for president. One problem was his age. Jack was forty-three. Some people thought that was too young. But many voters liked the idea of a young president. They saw that Jack was practically bursting with energy. He promised to "get the country moving."

Jack ran for president in 1960. Whenever he gave a speech, large crowds came to hear him.

A Secret

When Jack was thirty, doctors were finally able to tell him why he was sick so much. He had an illness called Addison's disease. Jack had to take medicine for the rest of his life. No one outside his family knew this, though. Jack and his family kept his illness a secret.

Jack's religion was another problem. He was Catholic. The leader of the Roman Catholic Church is the pope, who lives in Rome. The pope is in charge of Catholics all over the world. But some people thought that the pope shouldn't tell a president of the United States what to do. There had never been a Catholic president before. These people wanted to keep it that way.

Jack went on TV. He spoke about his religion. He stood up for his right to be president. After all, "nobody asked me if I was Catholic when I joined the United States Navy," he said.

At last, Jack was named the Democratic Party's choice for president. The Republican Party chose Richard Nixon. Jack would have to beat Nixon to become president.

Jack asked Nixon to take part in a debate. The two would discuss important issues face-to-face. The debate was the first ever on TV. Millions of people watched. Most of them thought that Nixon looked nervous. There were little beads of sweat on his upper lip. Jack, on the other hand, looked calm. He seemed sure of his answers. That's how a president should look, viewers said.

This family watches a debate between Jack Kennedy and Richard Nixon. Most people thought Jack looked good on TV.

On November 8, 1960, Americans voted. It was very close. But when all the votes were counted, Jack had made history. He was the youngest person—and the first Roman Catholic—ever elected president of the United States.

4 A PRESIDENT'S JOB

Jack and Jackie moved into the White House with their two children. Caroline was three years old. Her little brother, John Jr., was just a baby.

Right away, Jack started a program called the Peace Corps. Peace Corps volunteers went to poor countries. They taught school. And they taught people how to build roads and plant crops.

Peace Corps volunteers live in villages with the people they are trying to help. They learn the people's language and customs.

Soon thousands of Peace Corps volunteers were making friends for the United States around the world.

Sometimes Jack had to deal with countries that did not like the United States at all. The most powerful of these countries was the Soviet Union. The two countries were not at war. But they were not exactly at peace either. People called it a "Cold War." Jack had to make sure that the Cold War did not turn into a real war.

One morning, an assistant showed Jack some photographs. The pictures showed that the Soviet Union was putting missiles on the island of Cuba. Cuba was only ninety miles away from the United States. Jack knew that this was big trouble. A nuclear missile fired from Cuba could reach a U.S. city in minutes.

NUCLEAR WARHEAD BUNKER
UNDER CONSTRUCTION
SAN CRISTOBAL SITE 1

PREFABRICATION MATERIALS

A spy plane took this photo of a missile site the Soviet Union was building in Cuba.

Jack's advisers helped him decide what to do about the missiles in Cuba.

The missiles had to be taken away, Jack knew. But how could he make that happen? His advisers wanted him to send planes to attack Cuba. Destroy the missiles, they said. Of course, any Soviets working on the missiles would be killed. That was sure to start a nuclear war with the Soviet Union. A war like that had never been fought before. Half the people in the United States could die!

Instead, Jack decided to "quarantine" Cuba. U.S. Navy ships would surround the island and make a blockade. They would stop Soviet ships from reaching Cuba. The ships would not deliver more missiles.

Jack hoped that the blockade would prevent a deadly war. But no one was quite sure what the Soviets would do. They might become so angry that they would fire their missiles anyway. The blockade might start a war after all!

On October 24, 1962, the blockade began. Over 170 U.S. ships stood ready around Cuba. Soviet ships steamed toward them. What would happen when the two sides met? All Jack could do was wait.

"WE CHOOSE TO GO TO THE MOON"

Soon after Jack became president, the Soviets launched the first human in space. Jack didn't like coming in second to the Soviets. He made a decision. He promised that the United States would be first to land an astronaut on the Moon. The United States kept Jack's promise. On July 20, 1969, Neil Armstrong became the first person to walk on the Moon.

Before the missile crisis, Jack met with the leader of the Soviet Union. The two saw eye to eye on very little.

Suddenly, word came. The Soviet ships had stopped! They were not trying to cross the quarantine line. They were turning around. The blockade had worked!

Four days later, the Soviets agreed to remove the missiles from Cuba. Jack's gamble had paid off. The crisis was over.

Sometimes danger didn't come from other countries. Sometimes it came from the American people themselves.

In the South, black Americans were asking for more rights. They held marches in the streets. Some people didn't want black Americans to have the same rights that white Americans had. There were riots. Police dogs attacked the marchers. High-pressure hoses knocked them off their feet. Angry crowds insulted them.

Three civil rights protesters are sprayed with a high-pressure fire hose. Its spray is strong enough to tear the bark from trees.

In June 1963, two black students tried to enroll at the University of Alabama. The school had never had a black student before. The governor of Alabama himself tried to stop the students. He stood in the doorway of the school and would not let them pass. It was an ugly moment. Jack had to send soldiers to end the standoff. At last, the students were admitted.

Governor George Wallace blocks a doorway at the University of Alabama.

Jack told the American people that discrimination was wrong. But not everyone agreed with him.

That night, Jack spoke to the country on TV. He spoke plainly. He said that treating people differently because of the color of their skin was simply wrong. Doing so had no place in American law. It had no place in American life.

He told people that he was asking for new laws to be passed. The laws would make sure that all Americans—white or black—would be treated the same. But it was not enough to change the law, he said. He challenged the American people to change their minds. He challenged them to change their lives.

Martin Luther King Jr. spoke to more than 250,000 people during the March on Washington.

Two months after Jack's speech, there was another march for equality. This one was in Washington, D.C. Thousands of people gathered around the Lincoln Memorial. They cheered as they listened to speeches by black leaders. One of the speakers at the march was Martin Luther King Jr. He stirred everyone who heard him with his "I Have a Dream" speech. There were no riots—not even a fistfight. Everything was peaceful.

After the march, Jack invited the leaders to the White House. He shook their hands. When he shook King's hand, Jack said, "I have a dream." It was Jack's way of saying that he had been moved by King's speech too. He told the leaders how happy he was with the march. "You made the difference," one told him. "You gave us your blessings."

Civil rights leaders meet with Jack in the White House. King is third from the left.

5 DALLAS

Not everyone was happy with the job that Jack was doing. Some were angry at what he had done for black Americans. Others wanted him to be tougher on the Soviet Union.

A new election was coming up. Jack was determined to win. That meant he would have to convince the voters he was doing a good job.

Jack decided to start his election campaign in the South. On November 22, 1963, he and Jackie went to Dallas, Texas.

The crowd that greeted Jack's plane was anything but unhappy. People were jumping up and down in excitement. They screamed and cheered as if he were a rock star. Jack called it a "real Texas welcome."

Jack and Jackie receive a warm welcome in Dallas. Jackie carries a bouquet of red roses given to her upon her arrival.

Jackie greets an enthusiastic crowd in Dallas.

Jack and Jackie shook hands with some of the crowd. Then they stepped into an open car for the ride through Dallas. The governor of Texas and his wife joined them.

The streets of Dallas were lined with people—250,000 of them. They jostled each other to get glimpses of Jack and Jackie. They leaned out of windows for a better view. The roar of their cheers drowned out the sound of the motorcycles riding alongside Jack's car.

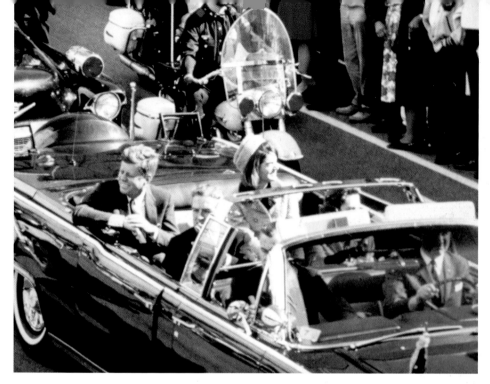

Jack and Jackie ride through the streets of Dallas.

Crack!

Suddenly, a sharp noise echoed through the streets. A car backfiring, thought some people. Firecrackers, thought others.

But they were wrong. The sound was a gunshot.

A bullet streaked over the heads of the crowd. It hit Jack. A moment later, another bullet followed. This one also struck him. Jack slumped to the side of his seat in the car.

The president had been shot! The car roared forward. It raced to the hospital. But it was too late. A short time later, the official word came. At age forty-six, John F. Kennedy was dead.

Radio and TV announcers told people what had happened. The nation was stunned by the horrible news. All over the country, people stopped what they were doing. For the rest of their lives, they would remember where they had been at that moment.

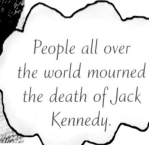

People all over the world mourned the death of Jack Kennedy.

HISTORY ON WHEELS

The car that Jack rode in was specially made for the president of the United States. Officially, it was called X-100. After Jack died, four more presidents used the car—Lyndon B. Johnson, Richard Nixon, Gerald Ford, and Jimmy Carter. In 1977, the car went to the Henry Ford Museum. It was put on display as a piece of United States history.

John F. Kennedy had been president for only 1,036 days. In that short time, he had made the country safer. He had set the nation on a new road to equal rights for black Americans. He had encouraged Americans to aim for the Moon and the stars. He had opened a door to a new future for the American people. But they would have to meet the future without him. John F. Kennedy was gone.

TIMELINE

In the year . . .

1935 John F. Kennedy graduated from high school.

1940 he graduated from Harvard in June.   Age 23
his book *Why England Slept* was published in August.

1941 he joined the U.S. Navy in October.
the United States entered World War II on December 8.

1943 *PT-109* was sunk on August 2.

1946 Jack was first elected to the U.S. House of   Age 29
Representatives.

1952 he was first elected to the U.S. Senate.

1953 he married Jacqueline Bouvier on September 12.

1956 his book *Profiles in Courage* was published.

1960 he was elected president of the United   Age 43
States.

1961 he created the Peace Corps.

1962 he announced a quarantine to end the Soviet shipment of missiles to Cuba.

1963 he announced new laws to give equal rights   Age 46
to black Americans in June.
he was killed in Dallas, Texas, on November 22.
he was awarded the Presidential Medal of Freedom by President Johnson in December.

WHO KILLED THE PRESIDENT?

L ee Harvey Oswald was arrested for killing President Kennedy. Two days later, he too was shot and killed. There was no trial. So there was no way to judge what had happened on November 22, 1963. Some people wondered whether or not Oswald really was the killer.

Over the years, people have pointed fingers at all sorts of suspects. Some said a group of criminals killed Kennedy. Others said it was spies from some foreign country. Some even said it was agents from the U.S. government itself.

No one has ever found anything to prove these stories. All the evidence points to Oswald. Still, some people continue to ask: Who really killed John F. Kennedy?

Lee Harvey Oswald (RIGHT) was shot as he was being moved to a different prison on November 24, 1963.

FURTHER READING

Anderson, Catherine Corley. *Jacqueline Kennedy Onassis: Woman of Courage.* Minneapolis: Lerner Publications Company, 1995. This biography tells the life story of the former First Lady.

Chrisp, Peter. *The Cuban Missile Crisis.* Milwaukee, WI: World Almanac, 2002. A good overview of the Cuban Missile Crisis.

Cooper, Ilene. *Jack: The Early Years of John F. Kennedy.* New York: Dutton Books, 2003. An account of Jack's childhood, accompanied by black-and-white photos.

Finlayson, Reggie. *We Shall Overcome: The History of the American Civil Rights Movement.* Minneapolis: Lerner Publications Company, 2003. A vivid history of the civil rights movement in the United States.

Hampton, Wilborn. *Kennedy Assassinated!: The World Mourns: A Reporter's Story.* Cambridge, MA: Candlewick Press, 1997. A behind-the-scenes look at the day Kennedy was assassinated.

Heiligman, Deborah. *High Hopes: A Photobiography of John F. Kennedy.* Washington, DC: National Geographic, 2003. A beautifully illustrated overview of Jack and his family.

Levine, Ellen. *Freedom's Children: Young Civil Rights Activists Tell Their Own Stories.* Madison, WI: Turtleback Books, 2001. Inspiring stories of children and teenagers who contributed to the civil rights movement.

WEBSITES

The White House: John Kennedy
<http://www.whitehouse.gov/history/presdents/jk35html>
Visitors to this website can learn about Jack's life.

The Peace Corps
<www.peacecorps.gov> Learn all about the Peace Corps at
this informative website, including where corps volunteers
work and what they do.

SELECT BIBLIOGRAPHY

Ballard, Robert D. "The Search for PT-109." *National
Geographic*, December 2002, 78–87.

Bishop, Jim. *The Day Kennedy Was Shot*. New York: Funk
& Wagnalls, 1968.

Dallek, Robert. "The Medical Ordeals of JFK." *Atlantic
Monthly*, December 2002, 49–61.

Hamilton, Nigel. *JFK: Reckless Youth*. New York: Random
House, 1992.

Kennedy, John F. *The Greatest Speeches of President John F.
Kennedy*. Bellingham, WA: Titan Publishing, 2001.

Kenney, Charles. *John F. Kennedy: The Presidential
Portfolio: History as Told through the Collection of the
John F. Kennedy Library and Museum*. New York:
PublicAffairs, 2000.

*Report of the President's Commission on the Assassination
of President Kennedy*. Washington, DC: U.S.
Government Printing Office, 1964.

INDEX

Acknowledgments

For photographs and artwork: The John F. Kennedy Library, pp. 4, 7, 9, 10, 11, 14, 17, 19, 21, 23, 29, 30, 32, 35, 37, 39, 40; © CORBIS, p 15; *The New Bedford Standard-Times*, p. 20; © Bettmann/CORBIS, pp. 22, 33, 42; National Archives, p. 25; The Peace Corps, p. 28; © HultonlArchive by Getty Images, p. 34; © Hulton-Deutsch Collection/CORBIS, p. 36; The Everett Collection, pp. 41, 45; Front Cover: John F. Kennedy Library; Back Cover: © David J. and Janice L. Frent Collection/CORBIS.
For quoted material: pp. 7, 16, Nigel Hamilton, *JFK: Reckless Youth* (New York: Random House, 1992); pp. 23, 24, 37, Charles Kenney, *John F. Kennedy: The Presidential Portfolio: History as Told through the Collection of the John F. Kennedy Library and Museum* (New York: PublicAffairs, 2000); p. 30, *John F. Kennedy, The Greatest Speeches of President John F. Kennedy* (Bellingham, WA: Titan Publishing, 2001); p. 37, Richard Reeves, *President Kennedy: Profile of Power* (New York: Simon & Schuster, 1993); p. 39, Jim Bishop, *The Day Kennedy Was Shot* (New York: Funk & Wagnalls, 1968).